30 MILLION DIFFERENT INSECTS IN THE RAINFOREST

PAUL ROCKETT

W

FRANKLIN WATTS
LONDON•SYDNEY

First published in 2014 by Franklin Watts

Franklin Watts
338 Euston Road
London NW1 3BH

Franklin Watts Australia
Level 17/207 Kent Street
Sydney, NSW 2000

Editor: Rachel Cooke
Design and illustration: Mark Ruffle
www.rufflebrothers.com

Dewey number: 595.7'09152
HB ISBN: 978 1 4451 2672 2
Library ebook: 978 1 4451 2678 4

Printed in China

Franklin Watts is a division of Hachette
Children's Books, an Hachette UK company.
www.hachette.co.uk

Picture credits: Adstock/Shutterstock: 17tl; Ryan M
Bolton/Shutterstock: front cover c.
Dirk Ercken/Shutterstock: 26tcr; Rui Ferreira/
Shutterstock: 25c; guentermanaus/Shutterstock:
15cl; Rob Hainer/Shutterstock: 26tcl; Hamster Man/
Shutterstock: 15cr; Hartl/blickwinkel/Alamy: 7br; Piter
Hason/Shutterstock: 17tlb; Steffen Hauser/botanikfoto/
Alamy: 17; Ron Haviv/VII/Corbis: 10bl; Anton Ivanov/
Shutterstock: 18bl; JBK/Shutterstock: 28br; Kjersti
Joergensen/Shutterstock: 19ccl; Wolfgang Kaehler/
Corbis: 8tl; Andrew Karivny/Shutterstock: 19cl;
Cynthia Kidwell/Shutterstock: 18br; Anna Kucherova/
Shutterstock: 18bcr; Lightpoet/Shutterstock: front
cover tr; Liquid Productions/LLC/Shutterstock:
15c; Alfredo Maiquez/Shutterstock: 26tr; Nagel
Photography/Shutterstock: 19cr; Nella/Shutterstock:
4cl; Leon P/Shutterstock: 18bcl; Al Pidgin/Shutterstock:
20cl; Poetic Penguin/Shutterstock: 19ccr; Alexander
Potapov/Shutterstock: 28bc; Mike Price/Shutterstock:
20tl; Dr Morley Read/Shutterstock: 4tl, 12bl, 14t,
26tl; David Reilly/Shutterstock: 17cl, 17clb, 17bl;
reptiles4all/Shutterstock: 26cl; worldswildlifewonders/
Shutterstock: 29tl, 29c; Pan Xunbin/Shutterstock: 17cla;
S Zefei/Shutterstock: front cover bcl.

Throughout the book you are given data relating
to various pieces of information covering the topic.
The numbers will most likely be an estimation based
on research made over a period of time and in a
particular area. Some other research may reach
a different set of data, and all these figures may
change with time as new research and information is
gathered. The numbers provided within this book are
believed to be correct at the time of printing and have
been sourced from the following sites:
allaboutwildlife.com; animalinfo.org; animals.
about.com; animals.howstuffworks.com; animals.
nationalgeographic.co.uk; answersingenesis.org;
archive.org; atbi.biosci.ohio-state.edu; a-z-animals.
com; baylor.edu ; biokids.umich.edu; chemistry.about.
com; celebratebrazil.com; ehow.co.uk; factsanddetails.
com; folklife.si.edu; ga.water.usgs.gov; gardenguides.
com; geointeractive.co.uk; gymmuenchenstein.ch;
independent.co.uk; iucnredlist.org; kidsbutterfly.
org; kids.mongabay.com; library.thinkquest.
org; link.springer.com; nature.org; oxfam.org.uk;
placesbook.org; planet.infowars.com; rain-tree.com;
rainforestconservation.org; rainforests.mongabay.
com; rainforestrescue.sky.com; rainforestsos.org;
redjellyfish.com; savetherainforest.org; science.
howstuffworks.com; si.edu; survivalinternational.
org; tolweb.org; wisegeek.org; worldbank.org;
worldfactsandfigures.com; worldlywise.blogspot.co.uk;
worldrainforestfoundation.org; wwf.org.uk; wwf.panda.
org.

CONTENTS

COUNTING DOWN THE RAINFOREST

What is a rainforest?

Rainforests are so-called because they are dense patches of forest that receive a large amount of rain.

THERE ARE TWO TYPES OF RAINFOREST:

○ TROPICAL

Tropical rainforests are found around the Equator and are constantly warm and humid.

● TEMPERATE

Temperate rainforests are found outside the Tropics, near coastlines, and experience colder weather than tropical rainforests.

Tropic of Cancer

Equator

Tropic of Capricorn

COUNTING THE RAINFORESTS

Within rainforests there are areas of land that have yet to be explored and a vast amount of wildlife that has yet to be discovered.

Scientists will estimate the number of creatures and plants within the rainforest. They do this because the amount of wildlife is too great to count individually and because a lot of rainforest life is still unknown.

An estimate is a prediction based upon experience and information available at that time. Estimates are used to demonstrate the size and variety of rainforest life, often to give an idea of what they contain within a scale that we might understand.

IT IS ESTIMATED THAT A 1 KM² AREA OF THE RAINFOREST CONTAINS AS MANY AS:

144 species of flowering plant
72 species of trees
39 species of bird
14 species of butterfly
12 species of mammal
10 species of reptile
8 species of amphibian.

These estimates are based on smaller areas of rainforest where the content is able to be counted.

1 KM

1 KM

WHAT IS A SPECIES?

Species refers to a type of being. If there are eight species of amphibian in **1 km²**, we don't mean that there are just eight amphibians, but eight different types of amphibians, of which there may be a varying number.

1 km² is an area that covers the same amount of space that is **1 km** in both width and length.

The Amazon rainforest area is **5,500,000 km²**.

1   2   3   4   5   6   7   8

30 MILLION DIFFERENT INSECTS IN THE RAINFOREST

There are more insects in the rainforest than anywhere else in the world. New species are being discovered all of the time. There are around **1,000,000** insects that have been officially recorded, but many scientists estimate that there are actually **30,000,000** different insect species just in the rainforests.

THERE ARE SEVEN INSECT GROUPS. THEY ARE:

DRAGONFLIES	GRASSHOPPERS AND LOCUSTS	ANTS	TRUE BUGS	BUTTERFLIES AND MOTHS	BEES AND WASPS	BEETLES

NUMBER OF SPECIES IN INSECT GROUPS

2,000
4,000
6,000
8,000
10,000
12,000
14,000
〰〰〰
50,000
100,000
150,000
200,000
250,000
300,000
350,000
400,000

TRUE BUGS?
All insects are often called 'bugs' but true bugs are a group of bugs that are different from other insects. The main difference is that they suck! They have a long tube-like beak through which they suck in food.

RAINFOREST STUDY
In a study of rainforest insects, **100 different species** of ant have been found living in one tree. **700 different species** of beetle have also been found in **one tree**.

10,000,000,000,000,000,000 (10 quintillion) individual insects alive at any one time.

There are **400,000,000** different species of beetle; **20,000** of these are longhorn beetles. The largest beetle in the world is the titan beetle, which is from the longhorn beetle family.

THE TITAN BEETLE
THE WORLD'S BIGGEST
BEETLE

Titan beetles live deep in some of the world's hottest tropical jungles. Adults can grow to as long as **16.7 cm**. Their jaws are strong enough to snap a pencil in half and cause damage to a person's flesh.

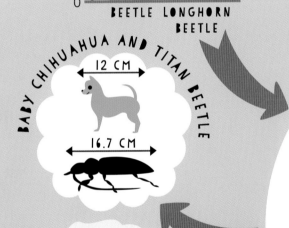

BABY CHIHUAHUA AND TITAN BEETLE

12 CM

16.7 CM

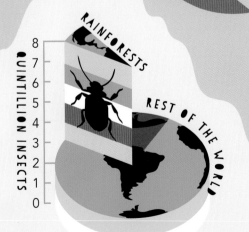

TITAN BEETLE

80% live in the rainforests. That means **8,000,000,000,000,000,000** (8 quintillion) individual insects live in **6%** of the world.

8,936,400 KM² OF THE WORLD IS TROPICAL RAINFOREST

Millions of years ago, the majority of the land on Earth was rainforest. 50,000,000 years ago Antarctica was warm enough to be considered as an area of rainforest, and is believed to have been covered with plant life. Today, Antarctica is the coldest place on Earth, so cold that no trees are able to grow there.

Archaeologists have uncovered fossils of wood and ferns from Antarctica that are not too different to those found in rainforests today.

RAINFORESTS ON EARTH 50,000,000 YEARS AGO

ANTARCTICA

The world has changed a lot over **50,000,000 years**. Areas of land have shifted, breaking up to become the countries and continents we now have. The world's climate has also changed, with the creation of different climate zones.

RAINFORESTS ON EARTH TODAY

Tropical rainforests have a tropical climate with an average temperature of **18°C**.

Antarctica is described as having a polar climate. The average temperature here is **−57°C**.

50
40
30
20
10
0
-10
-20
-30
-40
-50
-60

Earth's surface: **148,940,000 km²**

Today, all rainforests cover **8,936,400 km²** of the Earth's surface.

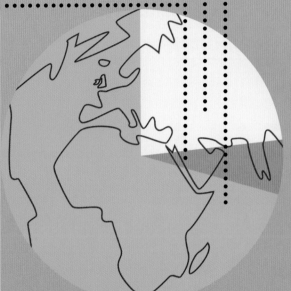

THE EARTH
Water: **70.8%**
Land: **29.2%**
Tropical rainforests: **6%**

6%

● Temperate rainforests cover **293,362 km²** of the Earth.

○ Tropical rainforests cover **8,643,038 km²** of the Earth.

THREE CLIMATE ZONES

The Earth's climates are affected by the movement and shape of the Earth. The curve of the Earth and the tilt on its axis as it rotates mean that some parts of the Earth receive more Sun than others. The temperatures of the wind and ocean currents also add to the conditions within each climate zone.

○ **TEMPERATE** climates have cold winters and mild summers with year-round rain.

○ **TROPICAL** climate zones are hot all year and some are also very wet.

○ **POLAR** climate zones are extremely cold and dry with long, dark nights.

9

700 THOUSAND
TRIBAL PEOPLE IN BRAZIL

Tribal people rely on natural resources for survival and can live in extreme environments that can be treacherous for those who have not grown up there. It's believed that there are still some tribes that remain undiscovered, and so the exact number of tribes and tribal people around the world is unknown.

IN THE RAINFORESTS OF BRAZIL THERE ARE ESTIMATED TO BE:

700,000
tribal people in

200
different tribes
speaking a total of

170
languages.

AMAZON RAINFOREST

THE YANOMAMI TRIBE
Population: **32,000**

The Yanomami are the largest tribe living in the Amazon rainforest. They have special reserves of land set aside for them so that they can continue their traditional existence. The land covers **23,722,120 acres** in Brazil (twice the size of Switzerland) and **20,509,750 acres** in Venezuela.

POPULATION OF SWITZERLAND:
7,909,000

YANOMAMI POPULATION:
32,000

THE AKUNTSU TRIBE

Population: 5

The Akuntsu are the smallest known tribe living in the Amazon rainforest. During the 1980s and '90s, the Akuntsu tribe suffered violent attacks by some land developers and now only five members remain. They live in a small patch of forest surrounded by huge cattle ranches and plantations, places that used to be home to their once large tribe.

TRIBAL THREATS

In Brazil alone **90 tribes** are known to have been wiped out.

The tribes live in harmony with the rainforest.

The tribes' land is destroyed by developers. Some attack the tribes and bring with them new germs and diseases.

With their habitat taken from them, and diseases and developers killing them, the tribes become extinct.

YANOMAMI TRIBE TIMELINE

50,000,000 years ago
The Yanomami tribe are believed to have been living in the Amazon rainforest for over **50,000,000 years**.

1940s
The Yanomami tribe were first discovered in the 1940s. Their encounter with people from the outside world led to many deaths from measles and 'flu.

1970s
In the 1970s bulldozers drove through their territory, building roads enabling the deforestation of their land.

1980s
In the 1980s **40,000 gold-miners** invaded their land. Many villages were destroyed and tribes people shot. **20%** of the Yanomami died in just **seven years** during this period.

1990s
In 1992, Brazil recognised the Yanomami tribe's right to land, marking an area as the 'Yanomami Park'. However, a year later outsiders invaded and killed many of the tribe.

2000s–2014
Over **1,000 gold-miners** are reported to be working illegally on Yanomami land. They are spreading diseases like malaria, and polluting the rivers and forests with mercury. The tribe's health is suffering and medical care is not immediately available to them.

HOW THEY LIVE

The Yanomami tribe live in large circular houses, some of which can house up to **400 people**. Men hunt for food, while women tend gardens and grow crops.

The Yanomami have a huge knowledge of plants within the rainforest and use about **500 plants** for food, medicine, house building and tools.

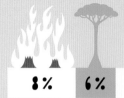

Today, tropical rainforests cover 6% of the Earth's land; 50 years ago they covered 14%.

8% 6%

100% LAND SURFACE

If this rate of disappearance were to continue, in another **50 years** there would be no rainforest left.

The removal of trees from the rainforest is called deforestation.

CAUSES OF DEFORESTATION:

Subsistence farming: **48%**
Commercial agriculture: **32%**
Logging: **14%**
Fuel wood removal: **5%**

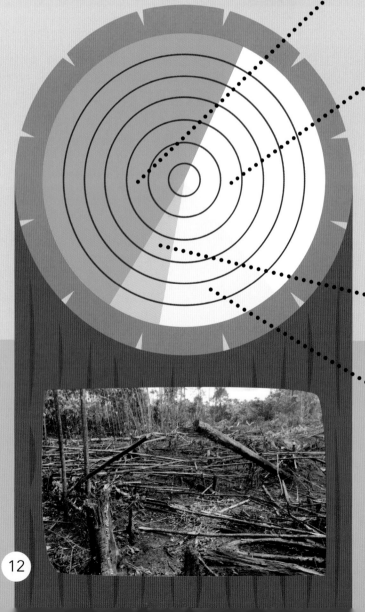

SUBSISTENCE FARMING is when farmers and tribes grow enough food to feed their immediate community. It involves a slash-and-burn technique of cutting down trees and burning forests. The land is only farmed for a short period of time before moving on to another area of land.

COMMERCIAL AGRICULTURE is when big companies develop land on a large scale to grow crops and graze cattle to sell. Single crops tend to be grown which removes the diversity of nutrients in the soil. Fertilisers are also used which pollute the soil.

Land is also cleared to keep and rear livestock, such as chickens and pigs, which will then be sold. In the Brazilian rainforests, land has been cleared for:

| 700 million chickens | 220 million cows | 60 million pigs | 20 million goats |

LOGGING is when trees are cut down and used for furniture and construction. Within the rainforest, large areas are destroyed to create access roads to logging sites and large trees are dragged over the forest floor.

FUEL WOOD REMOVAL is when trees are cut down for use as fuel. This is done on a large scale by mining and construction companies.

EFFECTS

The effects of all of these actions leave the rainforest soil dry and infertile. This makes it unlikely that any trees will be able to grow again on that land to replace the trees that were destroyed.

TO SCALE

To highlight the scale of destruction caused to the rainforests many reports refer to the size not in km² but with familiar objects and places. This may give us a better chance of understanding the actual scale.

AN AREA THE SIZE OF ENGLAND IS DESTROYED EACH YEAR.

A popular unit of measurement used when talking about rainforests is football pitches. The use of this unit is more for suggestive scale than accuracy. The difference in measurement between an American football pitch and a soccer pitch is small, so it could refer to either.

WITHIN THE TROPICAL RAINFORESTS:

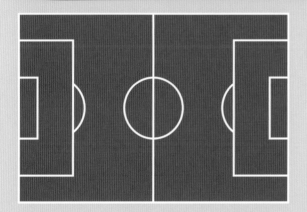

8,571,295 football pitches are destroyed each year.

23,483 football pitches a day.

1 ⅓ football pitch every five seconds.

The Earth is around **4,600,000,000 years old**. If we were to scale that to **46 years**, humans have been here for just **four hours** and the Industrial Revolution began just **one minute** ago.

In that time we've destroyed **50%** of the world's forests.

THE AMAZON RIVER IS 6,400 KM LONG

The Amazon river is the second longest river in the world.

The River Nile is the longest river, measuring **6,650 km**. The Amazon river is **6,400 km long**.

THE AMAZON RIVER HAS MORE TRIBUTARIES THAN ANY OTHER RIVER IN THE WORLD.

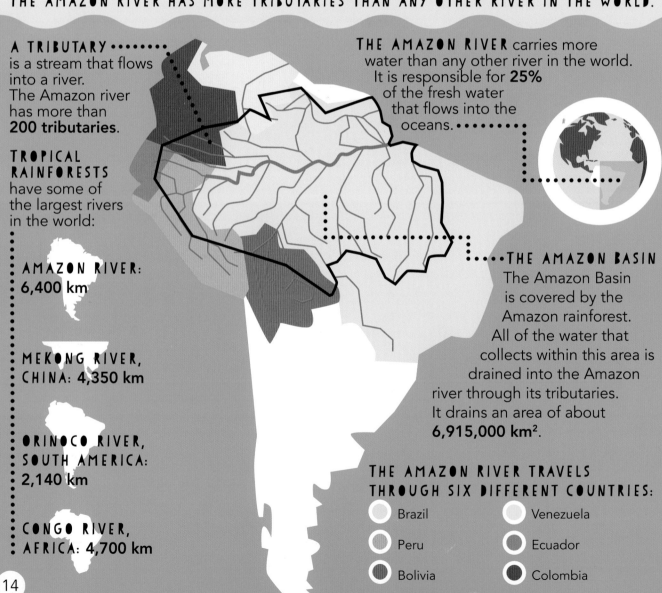

A TRIBUTARY ⋯⋯⋯ is a stream that flows into a river. The Amazon river has more than **200 tributaries**.

TROPICAL RAINFORESTS have some of the largest rivers in the world:

AMAZON RIVER: 6,400 km

MEKONG RIVER, CHINA: 4,350 km

ORINOCO RIVER, SOUTH AMERICA: 2,140 km

CONGO RIVER, AFRICA: 4,700 km

THE AMAZON RIVER carries more water than any other river in the world. It is responsible for **25%** of the fresh water that flows into the oceans. ⋯⋯⋯

THE AMAZON BASIN The Amazon Basin is covered by the Amazon rainforest. All of the water that collects within this area is drained into the Amazon river through its tributaries. It drains an area of about **6,915,000 km²**.

THE AMAZON RIVER TRAVELS THROUGH SIX DIFFERENT COUNTRIES:

- Brazil
- Venezuela
- Peru
- Ecuador
- Bolivia
- Colombia

LIFE IN THE RIVER

1,500 species of fish have been found in the Amazon river, but many more remain unidentified. The River Nile has just over **100 species of fish**.

 = 100 species

NILE

= **1,500 species**

AMAZON

The river is not just home to fish.
One of the largest crocodiles, the black caiman, lives there. They can grow up to **6 m** – that's over three times longer than a human!

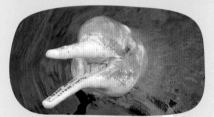

AMAZON RIVER DOLPHIN

WHAT IT EATS:

AMAZON MANATEE

WHAT IT EATS:

RED-BELLIED PIRANHA

WHAT IT EATS:

FOOD CHAIN

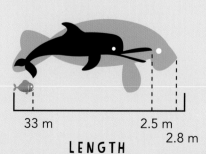

33 m   2.5 m
                  2.8 m

LENGTH

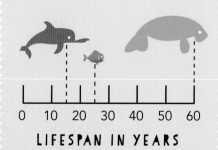

0 10 20 30 40 50 60

LIFESPAN IN YEARS

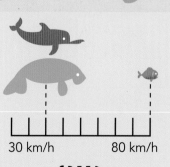

30 km/h   80 km/h

SPEED

3,000

EDIBLE FRUITS

There are at least 3,000 edible fruits in the tropical rainforests.

= 100 fruit

Tribes within the rainforest use over **2,000** fruit.

In the rest of the world only **200** of these fruits are used.

= 3,000 fruit

We eat many fruit, vegetables and nuts that originally came from tropical rainforests.

ORANGES **AVOCADOS** **PINEAPPLES** **PEPPERS** **FIGS** **NUTS**

100,000,000,000 bananas are eaten each year.

THE WORLD'S LARGEST PHARMACY

Around **25% of medicines** have been developed from tropical rainforest plants.

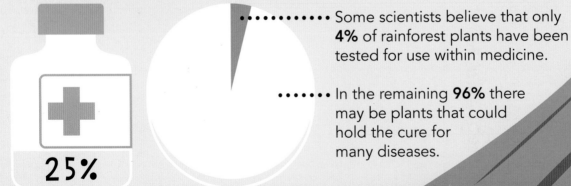

Some scientists believe that only **4%** of rainforest plants have been tested for use within medicine.

In the remaining **96%** there may be plants that could hold the cure for many diseases.

25%

THE KAPOK TREE

The kapok tree is one of the tallest trees in tropical rainforests. It is also one of the most useful plants. Every part of it is able to be used for different purposes.

THE SEED COVERING is used in pillows and mattresses.
SEED OIL from seeds is used as soap.

THE FLOWERS are edible raw and taste like marshmallow.

THE STAMENS are often added to curries and soups for colouring.

RESIN FROM THE LEAVES, SEEDS AND BARK is used to treat dysentery, asthma, fever and kidney disease.

MANY TRIBES USE THE TRUNK of the kapok tree to make canoes.

THE ROOTS can be eaten once roasted.

SEEDS

Most of the plants in the rainforest grow from a seed. When a plant produces a seed they often need to be scattered away from the mother plant to find space and food to grow.

There are many different ways that seeds travel around the rainforests.

Animals transport seeds on their fur and in their poo.

Some seeds fall into the river, floating and travelling to new locations.

The wind blows seeds off trees.

Some seeds explode out of plant pods, scattering over the ground.

17

260 DIFFERENT SPECIES OF MONKEY

The majority of the world's monkey species can be found in tropical rainforests. There are two main categories of monkey: New World monkeys and Old World monkeys. The main differences between the two groups are location and a prehensile tail.

WHAT IS A PREHENSILE TAIL?

A prehensile tail is a tail that is able to hold onto objects. New World monkeys have prehensile tails and are able to cling onto trees with them, whereas this ability is lacking in Old World monkeys – some Old World monkeys don't even have a tail.

NEW WORLD MONKEYS
They live in the rainforests of Central and South America.

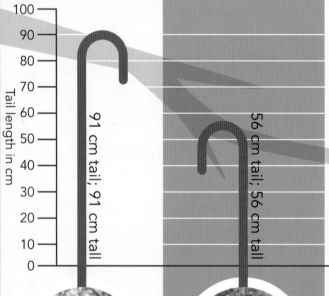

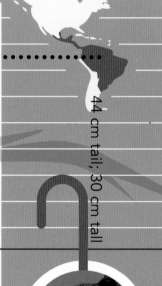

Tail length in cm

100 90 80 70 60 50 40 30 20 10 0

91 cm tail; 91 cm tall

56 cm tail; 56 cm tall

42 cm tail; 35 cm tall

44 cm tail; 30 cm tall

THE HOWLER MONKEY is so-called because it can make a howling noise that can be heard up to **4.8 km** away.

THE CAPUCHIN MONKEY lives almost all of its life up in the trees, only ever coming to the ground to find water. It can jump as far as **2.75 m** from tree to tree.

SQUIRREL MONKEYS are incredibly sociable animals hanging around in packs of **40** to **50**, although there has been a recorded sighting of a group numbering around **500**!

TAMARIN MONKEYS have distinctive facial hair, ranging from a white handlebar moustache to a full mane of golden hair.

OLD WORLD MONKEYS

They are found in Africa and Asia, but not all live in tropical rainforests; some live in grassland and some in mountainous areas that receive heavy snow.

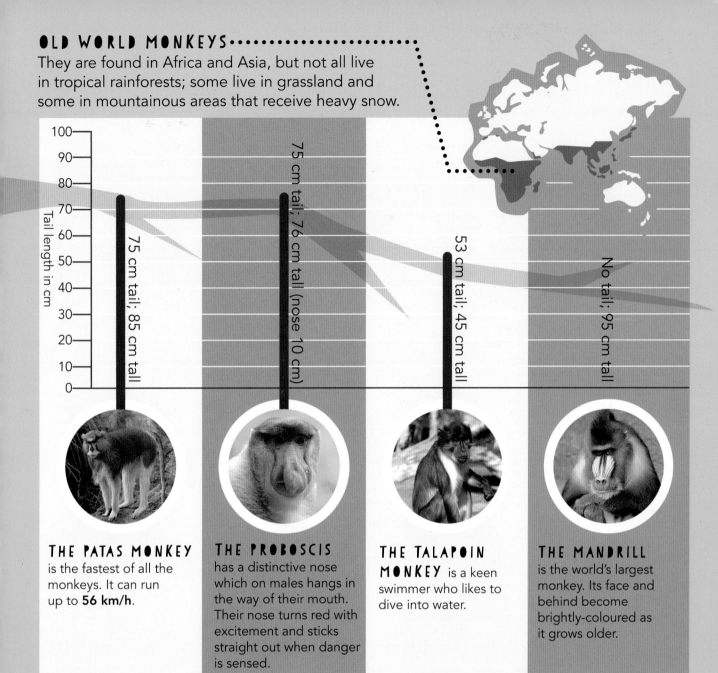

Tail length in cm

75 cm tail; 85 cm tall

75 cm tail; 76 cm tall (nose 10 cm)

53 cm tail; 45 cm tall

No tail; 95 cm tall

THE PATAS MONKEY is the fastest of all the monkeys. It can run up to **56 km/h**.

THE PROBOSCIS has a distinctive nose which on males hangs in the way of their mouth. Their nose turns red with excitement and sticks straight out when danger is sensed.

THE TALAPOIN MONKEY is a keen swimmer who likes to dive into water.

THE MANDRILL is the world's largest monkey. Its face and behind become brightly-coloured as it grows older.

MONKEYS AND GREAT APES

They may swing from the trees, but gorillas and lemurs are not monkeys. Humans are also not monkeys, but along with lemurs and gorillas, have evolved from the same branch of the evolutionary tree.

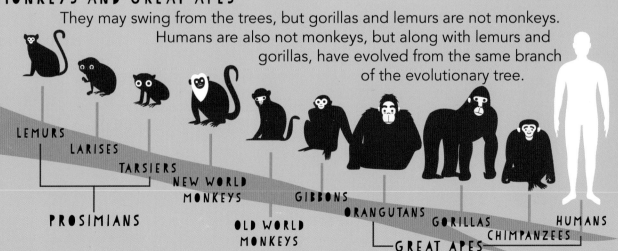

LEMURS

LARISES

TARSIERS

NEW WORLD MONKEYS

PROSIMIANS

OLD WORLD MONKEYS

GIBBONS

ORANGUTANS

GORILLAS

CHIMPANZEES

GREAT APES

HUMANS

137 PLANT, ANIMAL AND INSECT SPECIES DIE EACH DAY

Some experts estimate that 137 plant, animal and insect species are becoming extinct every day.

THAT'S OVER FIVE LIVING THINGS WIPED OUT EVERY HOUR.

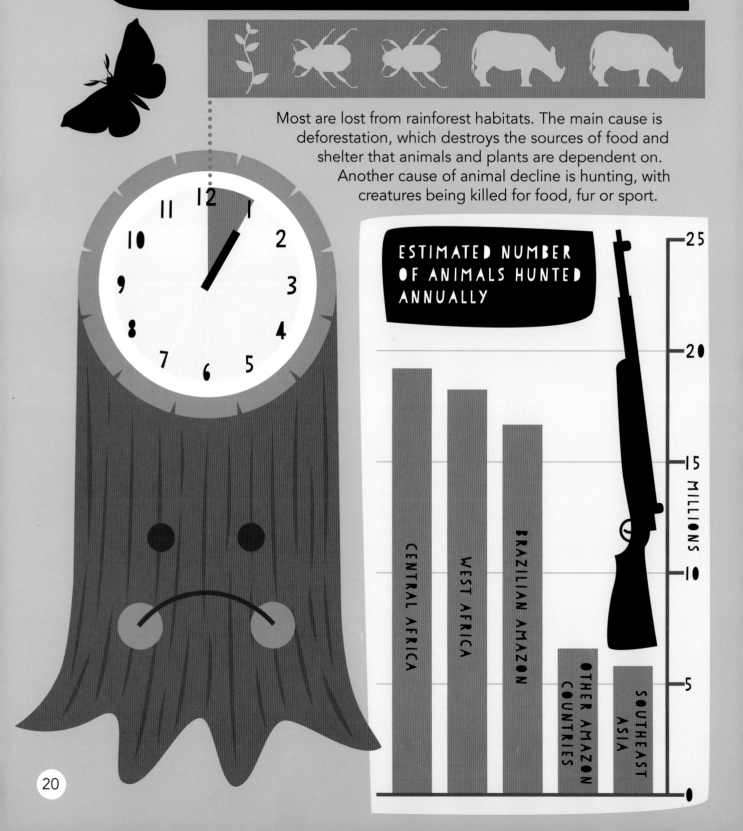

Most are lost from rainforest habitats. The main cause is deforestation, which destroys the sources of food and shelter that animals and plants are dependent on. Another cause of animal decline is hunting, with creatures being killed for food, fur or sport.

ESTIMATED NUMBER OF ANIMALS HUNTED ANNUALLY

MILLIONS

25

20

15

10

5

CENTRAL AFRICA

WEST AFRICA

BRAZILIAN AMAZON

OTHER AMAZON COUNTRIES

SOUTHEAST ASIA

CRITICALLY ENDANGERED ANIMALS

If a lifeform is critically endangered, it means that there are not many left and it is near extinction.

MOUNTAIN GORILLA

Weight: **220 kg**
Height: **1.8 m**

THREATS:
Deforestation: use of land for agriculture and trees for firewood
Hunting for meat, trophies
Human diseases
Illegal animal trade

Fewer than 820 mountain gorillas remain.

JAVAN RHINO

Fewer than 50 Javan rhinos remain.

Weight: **2,300 kg**
Length: **4 m**
Height: **1.7 m**

In October 2011, the last existing Javan rhino in Vietnam was found shot dead. The horn had been removed from the head. Many hunters view a rhino horn as a trophy. It is also used in some traditional Asian medicines. Rhino horn is said to be worth **$60,000 per kg**. That's over twice the price of gold. By 2031 all rhino species worldwide are expected to be extinct.

RIP

EXTINCT

DIGERUS GIBBERULUS
Died: 1996
A land snail that lived in the Brazilian rainforests.

SANTALUM FERNANDEZIUM
Died: 1908
A flowering tree that grew in the forests of India, Australia, South America and Indonesia.

GLAUCOUS MACAW
Died: 1994
A blue parrot from the South American rainforest.

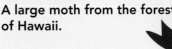

KONA GIANT LOOPER MOTH
Died: 1900s
A large moth from the forests of Hawaii.

88% HUMIDITY

Humidity refers to the amount of water vapour that is in the air. You can't see water vapour, but you can feel it. The more water vapour in the air, the more the air feels damp and wet.

100% HUMIDITY Wet, thick fog-like atmosphere

88% HUMIDITY Rainforest level of humidity

50% HUMIDITY Recommended humidity level for the home

0% HUMIDITY Completely dry

In the tropical rainforests the humidity level is high, this means that even when it isn't raining the atmosphere in the rainforest is always wet.

EARLY MORNING: The skies are clear and the air is cool. As the Sun rises, so too does the temperature.

LATE MORNING: It is very hot and water evaporates from the forest. As the hot air rises it cools and the water vapour condenses to form clouds.

MID AFTERNOON: Clouds are now full of moisture. A thunderstorm starts and there is a heavy downpour of rain.

EARLY EVENING: The storm is over and the air is cooler. The daily pattern is complete and ready to start again in the morning.

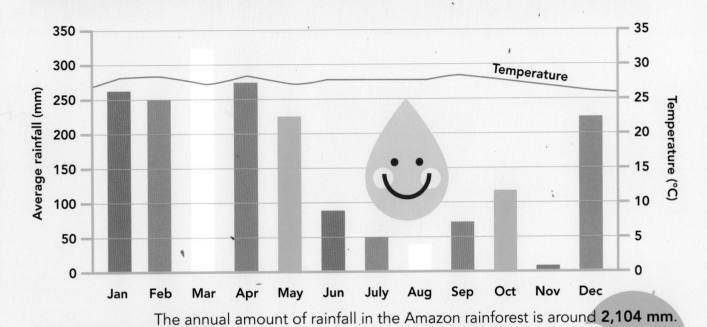

The annual amount of rainfall in the Amazon rainforest is around **2,104 mm**.

WATER CYCLE

The water cycle in the tropical rainforest means that water is either falling as rain or rising as water vapour. The water vapour rises through evaporation and transpiration.

EVAPORATION: this happens when the heat from the Sun turns water into vapour.

TRANSPIRATION: is when plants release water from their leaves, to help keep them cool.

SUN

CLOUD

CLOUD

HEAT FROM THE SUN

RAIN

10% TRANSPIRATION

Total water rising as vapour

••••••••90% EVAPORATION

28% OF THE WORLD'S OXYGEN

Tropical rainforests are often called the lungs of the world. They absorb carbon dioxide and recycle it into oxygen. However, micro-organisms on the floor of the oceans release a lot more oxygen into the world for us to breathe.

70% OXYGEN PRODUCED BY OCEAN FLOOR ORGANISMS

28% TROPICAL RAINFORESTS

2% OTHER

PHOTOSYNTHESIS

Oxygen comes from rainforest plants in a process called **photosynthesis**.

Plants use energy from the Sun to convert water and carbon dioxide from the air into sugar and oxygen.

LIGHT ENERGY FROM THE SUN

CARBON DIOXIDE FROM THE AIR

The green colour that you see in plants is created by a pigment called chlorophyll. Chlorophyll is able to capture energy from the Sun's light and use it to produce sugar. Plants use and store sugar as energy to help them grow. Animals eat the plants for their energy, which helps them to grow.

PHOTOSYNTHESIS COMES FROM THE GREEK:

PHOTO = LIGHT

SYNTHESIS =

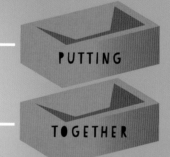

PUTTING

TOGETHER

OXYGEN

OXYGEN

SUGAR

CARBON DIOXIDE

WATER THROUGH THE ROOTS

OXYGEN

Oxygen is essential for living creatures. It is represented in science as the symbol O_2.

Oxygen is also present in water, which is represented as H_2O. A single fully-grown tree can release enough oxygen to support two human beings.

CARBON DIOXIDE

Humans and animals breathe out carbon dioxide. It is represented in science as the symbol CO_2. Too much carbon dioxide in the atmosphere is bad for the environment. Some scientists estimate that roughly **30%** of carbon dioxide released in the air comes from burning the rainforests.

THE GREENHOUSE EFFECT

The greenhouse effect is caused by greenhouse gases trapping the Sun's heat on Earth. Greenhouse gases include water vapour and carbon dioxide, which kept at certain levels make life possible on Earth. However, the large amounts of carbon dioxide produced by burning forests causes more heat to be trapped. As a result the average temperature on Earth rises. This has an impact on climate change, increasing the likelihood of droughts and the melting of the polar ice caps.

15-YEAR
LIFESPAN OF POISON DART FROG

Poison dart frogs are found in the rainforests of Central and South America.
Poison dart frogs are so-called because some South American tribes used to use the toxic secretions from the frogs to poison the tips of blow darts.

 In over **175 species**, only **three** were used for this purpose.

THEY ARE THE MOST TOXIC VERTEBRATE ON EARTH.

x 20,000

The golden poison dart frog from Colombia can produce enough toxins to kill **ten people** or **20,000 mice**. The equivalent of just two grains of table salt (less than **1 mg**), flowing in a person's bloodstream, can cause death in minutes.

It's believed that the poison is created by their particular diet of plants and insects. Those bred in captivity have a different diet, so are less poisonous.

The bright colours act as a warning to potential predators that they are dangerous to eat.

     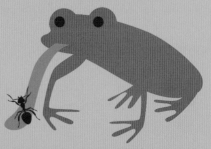

The poison dart frogs feed mostly on spiders, ants and termites, which they capture with their long sticky tongues.

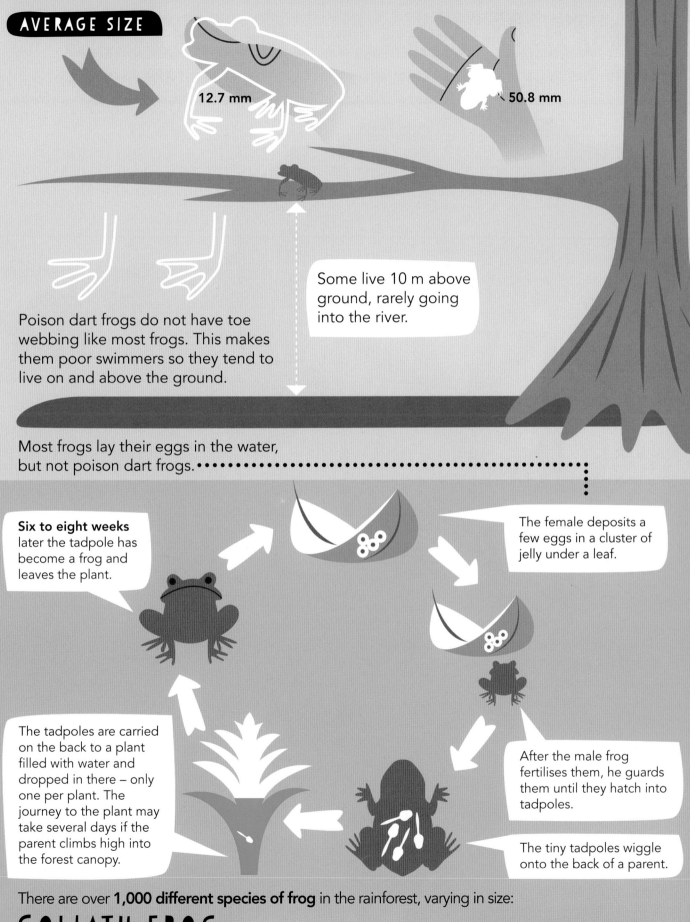

12.7 mm

50.8 mm

Some live 10 m above ground, rarely going into the river.

Poison dart frogs do not have toe webbing like most frogs. This makes them poor swimmers so they tend to live on and above the ground.

Most frogs lay their eggs in the water, but not poison dart frogs.

Six to eight weeks later the tadpole has become a frog and leaves the plant.

The female deposits a few eggs in a cluster of jelly under a leaf.

The tadpoles are carried on the back to a plant filled with water and dropped in there – only one per plant. The journey to the plant may take several days if the parent climbs high into the forest canopy.

After the male frog fertilises them, he guards them until they hatch into tadpoles.

The tiny tadpoles wiggle onto the back of a parent.

There are over **1,000 different species of frog** in the rainforest, varying in size:

GOLIATH FROG
33 cm

LEMUR LEAF FROG
3 cm

FOUR LAYERS OF THE RAINFOREST

The rainforest consists of four layers. Each layer has animal and plant life which are adapted to the conditions found there.

THE EMERGENT LAYER

contains a small number of trees that can grow up to **60 m**. Trees that grow into this layer have long straight trunks with branches that spread out wide at the top. Eagles, toucans, macaws and other birds can be seen flying in the treetops.

THE CANOPY

is the densest layer of the rainforest. Trees here can grow up to **45 m**.

THE AÇAÍ BERRY grows on the açaí palm tree and can be found in clumps hanging in the understory layer. The berry only stays ripe for approximately **24 hours**. If not eaten it will fall onto the forest floor.

DECOMPOSERS, such as termites, earthworms and fungi, inhabit the forest floor. Dead leaves fall here and are digested by the decomposers, releasing the nutrients they contain back into the soil. What may take one year to decompose in an average climate here takes six weeks.

THE HARPY EAGLE

lives in the emergent layer. It can live up to **35 years of age**. The eagle may swoop down into the canopy layer for food, and is partial to a nice bit of sloth.

The amount of **SUNLIGHT** each rainforest layer receives affects how much life lives there and how high and dense the plants are:

100% SUNLIGHT

EMERGENT: 60-45M

THE SLOTH lives in the canopy. It can live up to **30 years of age**. When it's feeling energetic, it reaches down into the understory to grab some açaí berries to eat slowly.

25% of all insect species can be found here

70-90% OF RAINFOREST LIFE LIVES IN THE CANOPY

95% SUNLIGHT

CANOPY: 45-20M

THE UNDERSTORY

is the bottom third of the total height of the rainforest. Plants in the understory can grow up to **20 m.**

5% SUNLIGHT

UNDERSTORY: 20-8M

FOREST FLOOR

This is where leaves and branches that fall from the trees are broken down by insects and fungi. Some small shrubs may grow up to **8 m.**

0.5% SUNLIGHT

FOREST FLOOR: 0-8M

FURTHER INFORMATION

BOOKS
Eco Alert! Rainforests by Rebecca Hunter (Franklin Watts, 2012)
Explore! Rainforests by Jen Green (Wayland, 2012)
River Adventures: Amazon by Paul Manning (Franklin Watts 2012)
Travelling Wild: Journey Along the Amazon by Alex Woolf (Wayland, 2013)

WEBSITES
Website containing information on the environmental issues surrounding tropical rainforests:
kids.mongabay.com/
Photos from the National Geographic with links to profiles on rainforest animals:
kids.nationalgeographic.co.uk/kids/photos/tropical-rainforests/
Games, activities and stories on the rainforest:
www.rainforest-alliance.org.uk/kids

Note to parents and teachers:
Every effort has been made by the publisher to ensure that these websites contain no inappropriate or offensive material. However, because of the nature of the Internet, it is impossible to guarantee that the content of these sites will not be altered. We strongly advise that Internet access is supervised by a responsible adult.

LARGE NUMBERS
1,000,000,000,000,000,000,000,000,000,000,000 = ONE DECILLION
1,000,000,000,000,000,000,000,000,000,000 = ONE NONILLION
1,000,000,000,000,000,000,000,000,000 = ONE OCTILLION
1,000,000,000,000,000,000,000,000 = ONE SEPTILLION
1,000,000,000,000,000,000,000 = ONE SEXTILLION
1,000,000,000,000,000,000 = ONE QUINTILLION
1,000,000,000,000,000 = ONE QUADRILLION
1,000,000,000,000 = ONE TRILLION
1,000,000,000 = ONE BILLION
1,000,000 = ONE MILLION
1000 = ONE THOUSAND
100 = ONE HUNDRED
10 = TEN
1 = ONE

GLOSSARY

amphibian	cold-bloodied vertebrate that lives both on land and in water
chlorophyll	a green pigment found in plants that is able to trap light from the Sun and convert it into sugar
climate	average weather conditions in a particular area
decomposers	organisms such as fungus and earthworms that break down and feed off dead plants and animals
deforestation	the cutting down and removal of trees in a forested area
dysentery	a disease characterised by diarrhoea that contains mucus and blood
endangered	at risk of extinction
equator	an imaginary line drawn around the Earth separating the Northern and Southern Hemispheres
estimate	an approximate calculation
evaporation	a process whereby a liquid becomes vapour
evolutionary tree	the idea that all life has grown into new lifeforms in the same way that a tree grows branches
extinct	having no living members; species that has died out
fertiliser	substance added to soil to increase plant growth
habitat	the environment or home of a creature or plant
humidity	amount of water vapour in the air
Industrial Revolution	a period when society began using machines and factories for producing goods, approximately between 1750–1850
infertile	not productive or able to produce life or grow plants
livestock	farm animals that are bought, sold and reared for commercial reasons
logging	the work of cutting down trees
malaria	an infectious disease that causes fevers carried by mosquitoes
mammal	warm-bloodied vertebrate
mercury	a silvery-white liquid metal
natural resources	material that is natural to the Earth and able to be used
nutrients	a substance that is beneficial to growth and well-being
photosynthesis	the process by which plants create their own food and produce oxygen
plantation	an area where a specific crop is grown on a large scale
prehensile	capable of grasping around an object
reptile	a cold-bloodied air-breathing vertebrate
reserve	a piece of land that has been set aside for a specific purpose
species	category of living things that contain shared characteristics
stamen	the fertilising organ of a plant
temperate	having a mild climate
toxic	a poisonous substance
transpiration	when water vapour is released from a plant
tributary	a river or stream that flows into a larger river
tropical	having a hot climate
vertebrate	a creature that has a spinal column
water vapour	water that at a certain temperature becomes invisible but is still felt as a wet element in the air

INDEX